LIFT EVERY VOICE

LIFT EVERY VOICE

Words of
Black Wisdom
and Celebration

Edited by Stephen Patterson
and S. M. Wu

BARNES
&NOBLE
B O O K S
NEW YORK

Acknowledgments

The editors wish to thank Rick Campbell, James DeMaiolo, Jack Henning, Adora Lam, Stuart Miller, Cathy Murphy, Brandon DeMaiolo Patterson, Katheryn Patterson, and Rhonda Winslow for their support, suggestions, and words of wisdom.

• • • •

Grateful acknowledgment is made to the following for permission to reprint their copyrighted material:

"From a Black Woman to a Black Man" by Maya Angelou. Copyright © 1995 by Maya Angelou. Reprinted by permission of The Helen Brann Agency, Inc.

"I, Too" by Langston Hughes. From COLLECTED POEMS by Langston Hughes. Copyright © 1994 by the Estate of Langston Hughes. Reprinted by permission of Alfred A. Knopf Inc.

"Our Time Has Come" by Jesse L. Jackson. Excerpted from Jesse L. Jackson's 1984 Address Before the Democratic National Convention. Reprinted by permission of the Reverend Jesse L. Jackson, President and Founder of The Rainbow Coalition, Inc.

"Lift Every Voice and Sing," copyright © 1917, 1921, 1935 by James Weldon Johnson, copyright renewed © 1963 by Grace Nail Johnson, from SAINT PETER RELATES AN INCIDENT by James Weldon Johnson. Used by permission of Viking Penguin, a division of Penguin Putnam Inc.

"I Have a Dream" by Martin Luther King Jr. Copyright © 1963 by Martin Luther King Jr., copyright renewed 1991 by Coretta Scott King. Reprinted by arrangement with The Heirs to the Estate of Martin Luther King Jr. c/o Writers House, Inc. as agent for the proprietor.

2000 Barnes & Noble Books

Book design by Kevin McGuinness
All illustrations copyright © 2000 by Kevin McGuinness
Images copyright © 1999 PhotoDisc, Inc.

ISBN 0-7607-1944-6 (*casebound*)
ISBN 0-7607-1945-4 (*paperback*)

Printed and bound in the United States of America

00 01 02 03 04 MC 9 8 7 6 5 4 3 2
00 01 02 03 04 MP 9 8 7 6 5 4 3 2 1
RRD-C

Contents

Introduction

LIFT EVERY VOICE is a treasury of inspirational words, sayings, and writings by people of color. These words of wisdom and enlightenment span generations, expressing the heritage of the past, the challenges of the present, and the promise of the future. Take a moment to hear these voices and what they have in common. Take the time to hear the echo of these voices in the halls of injustice. Take the time to hear the words of the past as they ring true today.

Lift ev'ry voice . . . We lift our voices to stifle the pain. We lift our voices to bring forth unbridled strength. We lift our voices because we know no other way. With our heads heavenward, we lift our voices and forge ahead.

There is no doubt that words written or spoken can resound as loud as the rolling sea. Even in this age of advanced communication and high technology, the *power* is still in the spoken and written word. Words are the most powerful instrument of all, whether whispered in a shack, scrawled in anger on a wall, born out of love on a scrap of paper, cooed from a baby's crib, wailed from behind bars, or shouted down the aisle at church on Sunday morning. In *Lift Every Voice*, words take these many shapes and forms.

You will find poetry here as well as excerpts from autobiographies, political speeches, and essays. Hear Sojourner Truth call out, "Ain't I a woman?" in her acclaimed incendiary speech to the Ohio Women's Rights Convention in 1851. Hear Henry M. Turner's choleric response of "Am I a man?" in his speech to the Georgia Legislature more than a decade later. Learn of the struggles of the past that continue today through the evocative and haunting poem "From a Black Woman to a Black Man," read by its author, Maya Angelou, at the Million Man March. Witness Jesse Jackson's challenge to today's youth in his speech to the 1984 Democratic National Convention in "Our Time Has Come."

Because inspirational words can come in small packages as well as large, you will also discover gem-like quotes surrounding the longer pieces. These quotes come from such figures as legendary singers James Brown and Billie Holliday, groundbreaking athletes Arthur Ashe and Michael Jordan, and thought-provoking political leaders Malcolm X and Shirley Chisholm. In their simplicity you will find complexity. Some of the quotes were chosen for their eloquence, some for their influence, some for their uniqueness, and some for their pure creativity and imagination. And some simply because they're fun for the soul.

Lift Every Voice is not only a chorus about identity, it's also a shout for inclusion. As the contributors come in many shades of brown, so too do they break through the range of political, professional, and religious ideologies. Recognize *yourself* in the diverse voices included in this collection.

Lift Every Voice is a rousing challenge, a dare. As we enter the new millennium, dare to lift up your voice to join those who have preceded you, to join those who lifted theirs—for they could not do otherwise.

—STEPHEN PATTERSON AND S. M. WU
NEW YORK CITY, 1999

Lift Every Voice and Sing
James Weldon Johnson

Lift ev'ry voice and sing,
Till earth and heaven ring,
Ring with the harmonies of Liberty;
Let our rejoicing rise,
High as the list'ning skies,
Let it resound loud as the rolling sea.

Sing a song full of the faith that the dark past
  has taught us,
Sing a song full of the hope that the present
  has brought us;
Facing the rising sun of our new day begun,
Let us march on till victory is won.

Stony the road we trod,
Bitter the chast'ning rod,
Felt in the days when hope unborn had died;
Yet with a steady beat,
Have not our weary feet,
Come to the place for which our fathers sighed?
We have come over a way that with tears has
  been watered.
We have come, treading our path thro' the
  blood of the slaughtered,
Out from the gloomy past,
Till now we stand at last
Where the white gleam of our bright star is cast.

God of our weary years,
God of our silent tears,
Thou who has brought us thus far on the way;
Thou who hast by Thy might,
Led us into the light,
Keep us forever in the path, we pray.
Lest our feet stray from the places, our God,
    where we met Thee,
Lest our hearts, drunk with the wine of the world,
    we forget Thee;
Shadowed beneath Thy hand,
May we forever stand,
True to our God,
True to our native land.

Schoolteachers **James Weldon Johnson** (1871-1938) and J. Rosamond Johnson (1873-1954) wrote the unofficial Negro National Anthem originally for schoolchildren to sing in celebration of Abraham Lincoln's birthday in 1900. Twenty years later, while working with the NAACP, James Weldon began to encourage the singing of the song at meetings throughout the country. The African American National Anthem continues to uplift and inspire to this day.

Say it loud

I'm Black and loud

proud!

I'm

—JAMES BROWN, *"The Godfather of Soul"*

For where does one run to when he's already in the promised land?

—**Claude Brown**, *writer*
from the Foreword to ***Manchild in the Promised land***

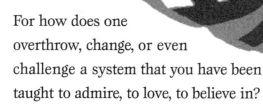

For how does one
overthrow, change, or even
challenge a system that you have been
taught to admire, to love, to believe in?

—**bell hooks**, *philosopher*

I, Too
Langston Hughes

I, too, sing America.

I am the darker brother.
They send me to eat in the kitchen
When company comes,
But I laugh,
And eat well,
And grow strong.

To-morrow,
I'll be at the table
When company comes.
Nobody'll dare
Say to me,
"Eat in the kitchen,"
Then.

Besides,
They'll see how beautiful I am
And be ashamed,—

I, too, am America.

James Mercer Langston Hughes (1902-1967) has often been called
the poet laureate of Harlem and one of the great talents of the
Harlem Renaissance. Poet, war correspondent, lyricist, librettist, news-
paper columnist, and author, he gave eloquent voice to a people barely
seen and rarely heard.

We black folk, our history and our present being, are a mirror of all the manifold experiences of America. What we want, what we represent, what we endure is what America is.

—**Richard Wright**, *writer*

This land is ours because we come out of it, we bled in it, our tears watered it, we fertilized it with our dead. So the more of us they destroy the more it becomes filled with the spirit of our redemption.

—**Ralph Ellison**, *writer*
from *Juneteenth*

I am America.
I am the part
you won't recognize.
But get used to me.
Black confident, cocky;
my name, not yours;
my religion, not yours;
my goals, my own;
get used to me.

—MUHAMMAD ALI, *prize fighter*

I know why the

Sympathy
Paul Laurence Dunbar

I know what the caged bird feels, alas!
    When the sun is bright on the upland slopes;
When the wind stirs soft through the springing grass,
And the river flows like a stream of glass;
    When the first bird sings and the first bud opes,
And the faint perfume from its chalice steals—
I know what the caged bird feels!

I know why the caged bird beats his wing
    Till its blood is red on the cruel bars;
For he must fly back to his perch and cling
When he fain would be on the bough a-swing;
    And a pain still throbs in the old, old scars

caged bird sings!

And they pulse again with a keener sting—
I know why he beats his wing!

I know why the caged bird sings, ah me,
    When his wing is bruised and his bosom sore,—
When he beats his bars and he would be free;
It is not a carol of joy or glee,
    But a prayer that he sends from his heart's deep core,
But a plea, that upward to Heaven he flings—
I know why the caged bird sings!

—1899

Poet-novelist **Paul Laurence Dunbar** (1872-1906) was born of former slaves, yet became the world's preeminent voice of African American poetry during his brief life. What better legacy than to inspire future writers such as Pulitzer Prize-winner Maya Angelou, whose autobiographical work takes its title from the last line of this poem.

There's only one way to be free. It's not something that someone gives you. It's something you take . . . and if you can't take it then you don't deserve it.

—**Malcolm X**, *civil rights leader*

The artist must elect to fight for freedom or slavery. I have made my choice. I had no alternative.

—Paul Robeson, *actor*

EXCERPT FROM

Up from Slavery
Booker T. Washington

Founder of the Tuskegee Normal and Industrial Institute in 1881, **Booker Taliaferro Washington** (1856-1915) was an educator as well as a political activist. He believed that through education, hard work, and self-reliance black Americans could liberate themselves from slavery's binding legacy.

Chapter I — A Slave Among Slaves

I was born a slave on a plantation in Franklin County, Virginia. I am not quite sure of the exact place or exact date of my birth, but at any rate I suspect I must have been born somewhere and at some time. As nearly as I have been able to learn, I was born near a cross-roads post-office called Hale's Ford, and the year was 1858 or 1859. I do not know the month or the day. The earliest impres-

"My life had its beginning in the midst of the most miserable, desolate, and discouraging surroundings."

sions I can now recall are of the plantation and the slave quarters—the latter being the part of the plantation where the slaves had their cabins.

My life had its beginning in the midst of the most miserable, desolate, and discouraging surroundings. This was so, however, not because my owners were especially cruel, for they were not, as compared with many others. I was born in a typical log cabin, about fourteen by sixteen feet square. In this cabin I lived with my mother and a brother and sister till after the Civil War, when we were all declared free.

Of my ancestry I know almost nothing. In the slave quarters, and even later, I heard whispered conversations among the coloured people of the tortures which the slaves, including, no doubt, my ancestors on my mother's side, suffered in the middle passage of the slave ship while being conveyed from Africa to America. I have been unsuccessful in securing any information that would throw any accurate light upon the history of my family beyond my mother. She, I remember, had a half-brother and a half-sister. In the days of slavery not very much attention was given to family history and family records—that is, black family records. My mother, I suppose, attracted the attention of a purchaser who was afterward my owner and hers. Her addition to the slave family attracted about as much attention as the purchase of a new horse or cow. Of my father I know even less than of my mother. I do not even know his name. I have heard reports to the effect that he was a white man who lived on one of the near-by plantations. Whoever he was, I never heard of his taking the least interest in me or providing in any way for my rearing. But I do not find especial fault with him. He was simply another unfortunate victim of the institution which the Nation unhappily had engrafted upon it at that time.

The cabin was not only our living-place, but was also used as the kitchen for the plantation. My mother was the plantation cook. The cabin was without glass windows; it had only openings in the side which let in the light, and also the cold, chilly air of winter. There was a door to the cabin—that is, something that was called a door—but the uncertain hinges by which it was hung, and the large cracks in it, to say nothing of the fact that it was too small, made the room a very uncomfortable one.

*   *   *

The early years of my life, which were spent in the little cabin, were not very different from those of thousands of other slaves. My mother, of course, had little time in which to give attention to the training of her children during the day. She snatched a few moments for our care in the early morning before her work began, and at night after the day's work was done. One of my earliest recollections is that of my mother cooking a chicken late at night, and awakening her children for the purpose of feeding them. How or where she got it I do not know. I presume, however, it was procured from our owner's farm. Some people may call this theft. If such a thing were to happen now, I should condemn it as theft myself. But taking place at the time it did, and for the reason that it did, no one could ever make me believe that my mother was guilty of thieving. She was simply a victim of the system of slavery. I cannot remember having slept in a bed until after our family was declared free by the Emancipation Proclamation. Three children—John, my older brother, Amanda, my sister, and myself—had a pallet on the dirt floor, or, to be more correct, we slept in and on a bundle of filthy rags laid upon the dirt floor.

I cannot remember a single instance during my childhood or early boyhood when our entire family sat down to the table together, and God's blessing was asked, and the family ate a meal in a civilized manner. On the plantation in Virginia, and even later, meals were gotten by the children very much as dumb animals get theirs. It was a piece of bread here and a scrap of meat there. It was a cup of milk at one time and some potatoes at another. Sometimes a portion of our family would eat out of the skillet or pot, while some one else would eat from a tin plate held on the knees, and often using nothing but the hands with which to hold the food. When I had grown to sufficient size, I was required to go to the "big house" at meal-times to fan the flies from the table by means of a large set of paper fans operated by a pulley. Naturally much of the conversation of the white people turned upon the subject of freedom and the war, and I absorbed a good deal of it. I remember that at one time I saw two of my young mistresses and some lady visitors eating ginger-cakes, in the yard. At that time those cakes seemed to me to be absolutely the most tempting and desirable things that I had ever seen; and I then and there resolved that, if I ever got free, the height of my ambition would be reached if I could get to the point where I could secure and eat ginger-cakes in the way that I saw those ladies doing.

*　　*　　*

The most trying ordeal that I was forced to endure as a slave boy, however, was the wearing of a flax shirt. In the portion of Virginia where I lived it was common to use flax as part of the clothing for the slaves. That part of the flax from which our clothing was made was largely the refuse, which of course was the cheapest and roughest part. I can scarcely imagine any torture, except, perhaps, the pulling of a tooth, that is equal to that caused by putting on a new flax shirt for the first time. It is almost equal to the feeling that one would experience if he had a dozen or more chestnut burrs, or a hundred small pin-points, in contact with his flesh. Even to this day I can recall accurately the tortures that I underwent when putting on one of these garments. The fact that my flesh was soft and tender added to the pain. But I had no choice. I had to wear the flax shirt or none; and had it been left to me to choose, I should have chosen to wear no covering.

*　　*　　*

I pity from the bottom of my heart any nation or body of people that is so unfortunate as to get entangled in the net of slavery. I have long since ceased to cherish any spirit of bitterness against the Southern white people on account of the enslavement of my race. No one section of our country was wholly responsible for its introduction, and, besides, it was recognized and protected for years by the General Government. Having once got its tentacles fastened on to the economic and social life of the Republic, it was no easy matter for the

"I pity from the bottom of my heart any nation or body of people that is so unfortunate as to get entangled in the net of slavery."

country to relieve itself of the institution. Then, when we rid ourselves of prejudice, or racial feeling, and look facts in the face, we must acknowledge that, notwithstanding the cruelty and moral wrong of slavery, the ten million Negroes inhabiting this country, who themselves or whose ancestors went through the school of American slavery, are in a stronger and more hopeful condition, materially, intellectually, morally, and religiously, than is true of an equal number of black people in any other portion of the globe. This is so to such an extent that Negroes in this country, who themselves or whose forefathers went through the school of slavery, are constantly returning to Africa as missionaries to enlighten those who remained in the fatherland. This I say, not to justify slavery—on the other hand, I condemn it as an institution, as we all know that in America it was established for selfish and financial reasons, and not from a missionary motive—but to call attention to a fact, and to show how Providence so often uses men and institutions to accomplish a purpose. When persons ask me in these days how, in the midst of what sometimes seem hopelessly discouraging conditions, I can have such faith in the future of my race in this country, I remind them of the wilderness through which and out of which, a good Providence has already led us....

—1901

Sometimes you have to give a little in order to get a lot.

—**Shirley Chisholm,** *first black congresswoman*

Sometimes, I feel discriminated against, but it does not make me angry. It merely astonishes me. How *can* any deny themselves the pleasure of my company! It's beyond me.

—Zora Neale Hurston, *writer*

[T]he brutality in our history has always been redeemed by the peacemakers, the idealists, and the martyrs who—through bravery or humor or both—inevitably climb over the fences that intrude upon shared human connections.

—**Stanley Crouch**, *writer*

Had I lived the life
that the state planned
for me from the beginning,
I would have lived and died
in somebody else's kitchen,
or somebody else's land,
and never written a word.
That knowledge is bone deep,
and it informs everything I do.

—TONI MORRISON,
Nobel Prize-winning writer

"Letter to My Old Master"
(excerpt from Letter to Thomas Auld)
Frederick Douglass

Frederick Douglass (1817-1895) has been called the most important African American leader of the nineteenth century. Often heralded as the "Father of the Civil Rights Movement," Douglass was born a slave but died a free man respected around the world.

Thomas Auld:

Sir — . . . I have selected this day on which to address you, because it is the anniversary of my emancipation; and knowing of no better why, I am led to this as the best mode of celebrating that truly important event. Just ten years ago this beautiful September morning, yon bright sun beheld me a slave—a poor, degraded chattel—trembling at the sound of your voice, lamenting that I was a man, and wishing myself a brute. The hopes which I had treasured up for weeks of a safe and successful escape from your grasp, were powerfully confronted at this last hour by dark clouds of doubt and fear, making my person shake and my bosom to heave with the heavy contest between hope and fear, I have no words to describe to you the deep agony of soul which I experienced on that never to be forgotten morning—(for I left by daylight). I was making a leap in the dark. The probabilities, so far as I could

"I am your fellow man, but not your slave"

by reason determine them, were stoutly against the undertaking. The preliminaries and precautions I had adopted previously, all worked badly. I was like one going to war without weapons—ten chances of defeat to one of victory. One in whom I had confided, and one who had promised me assistance, appalled by fear at the trial hour, deserted me, thus leaving the responsibility of success or failure solely with myself. You, sir, can never know my feelings. As I look back to them, I can scarcely realize that I have passed through a scene so trying. Trying however as they were, and gloomy as was the prospect, thanks be to the Most High, who is ever the God of the oppressed, at the moment which was to determine my whole earthly career. His grace was sufficient, my mind was made up. I embraced the golden opportunity, took the morning tide at the flood, and a free man, young, active and strong, is the result.

*　　*　　*

Since I left you, I have had a rich experience. I have occupied stations which I never dreamed of when a slave. Three out of the ten years since I left you, I spent as a common laborer on the wharves of New Bedford, Massachusetts. It was there I earned my first free dollar. It was mine. I could spend it as I pleased. I could buy hams or herring with it, without asking any odds of any body. That was a precious dollar to me. You remember when I used to make seven or eight, or even nine dollars a week in Baltimore, you would take every cent of it from me every Saturday night, saying that I belonged to you, and my earnings also. I never liked this conduct on your part—to say the best, I thought it a little mean. I would not have served you so. But let that pass.

✳   ✳   ✳

I married soon after leaving you: in fact, I was engaged to be married before I left you; and instead of finding my companion a burden, she was truly a helpmeet. She went to live at service, and I to work on the wharf, and though we toiled hard the first winter, we never lived more happily. After remaining in New Bedford for three years, I met with Wm. Lloyd Garrison, a person of whom you have *possibly* heard, as he is pretty generally known among slaveholders. He put it into my head that I might make myself serviceable to the cause of the slave by devoting a portion of my time to telling my own sorrows, and those of other slaves which had come under my observation. This was the commencement of a higher state of existence than any to which I had ever aspired. I was thrown into society the most pure, enlightened and benevolent that the country affords. Among these I have never forgotten you, but have invariably made you the topic

"I am your fellow man, but not your slave"

of conversation—thus giving you all the notoriety I could do. I need not tell you that the opinion formed of you in these circles, is far from being favorable. They have little respect for your honesty, and less for your religion.

But I was going on to relate to you something of my interesting experience. I had not long enjoyed the excellent society to which I have referred, before the light of its excellence exerted a beneficial influence on my mind and heart. Much of my early dislike of white persons was removed, and their manners, habits and customs, so entirely unlike what I had been used to in the kitchen-quarters on the plantations of the South, fairly charmed me, and gave me a strong disrelish for the coarse and degrading customs of my former condition. I therefore made an effort so to improve my mind and deportment, as to be somewhat fitted to the station to which I seemed almost providentially called. The transition from degradation to respectability was indeed great, and to get from one to the other without carrying some marks of one's former condition, is truly a difficult matter. I would not have you think that I am now entirely clear of all plantation peculiarities, but my friends here, while they entertain the strongest dislike to them, regard me with that charity to which my past life somewhat entitles me, so that my condition in this respect is exceedingly pleasant. So far as my domestic affairs are concerned, I can boast of as comfortable a dwelling as your own. I have an industrious and neat companion, and four dear children—the oldest a girl of nine years, and three fine boys, the oldest eight, the next six, and the youngest four years old. The three oldest are now going regularly to school—two can read and write, and the other can spell with tolerable correctness words of two syllables: Dear fellows! they are all in comfortable beds, and are sound asleep, perfectly secure under my own roof. There are no slaveholders here to rend my heart by snatching them from my arms, or blast a mother's dearest hopes by tearing them from her bosom. These dear children are ours—not to work up into rice, sugar and tobacco, but to watch over, regard, and protect, and to rear them up in the nurture and admonition of the gospel—to train them up in the paths of wisdom and virtue, and, as far as we can to make them useful to the world and to themselves. Oh! sir, a slaveholder never appears to me so completely an agent of hell, as when I think of and look upon my dear children. It is then that my feelings rise above my control. I meant to have said more with respect to my own prosperity and happiness, but thoughts and feelings which this recital has quickened unfit me to proceed further

"I am your fellow man, but not your slave"

in that direction. The grim horrors of slavery rise in all their ghastly terror before me, the wails of millions pierce my heart, and chill my blood. I remember the chain, the gag, the bloody whip, the death-like gloom overshadowing the broken spirit of the fettered bondman, the appalling liability of his being torn away from wife and children, and sold like a beast in the market. Say not that this is a picture of fancy. You well know that I wear stripes on my back inflicted by your direction; and that you, while we were brothers in the same church, caused this right hand, with which I am now penning this letter, to be closely tied to my left, and my person dragged at the pistol's mouth, fifteen miles, from the Bay side to Easton to be sold like a beast in the market, for the alleged crime of intending to escape from your possession. All this and more you remember, and know to be perfectly true, not only of yourself, but of nearly all of the slaveholders around you.

At this moment, you are probably the guilty holder of at least three of my own dear sisters, and my only brother in bondage. These you regard as your property. They are recorded on your ledger, or perhaps have been sold to human flesh mongers, with a view to filling your own ever-hungry purse. Sir, I desire to know how and where these dear sisters are. Have you sold them? or are they still in your possession? What has become of them? are they living or dead? And my dear old grandmother, whom you turned out like an old horse, to die in the woods—is she still alive? Write and let me know all about them. If my grandmother be still alive, she is of no service to you, for by this time she must be nearly eighty years old—too old to be cared for by one to whom she has ceased to be of service, send her to me at Rochester, or bring her to Philadelphia, and it shall be the crowning happiness of my life to take care of her in her old age. Oh! she was to me a mother, and a father, so far as hard toil for my comfort could make her such. Send me my grandmother! that I may watch over and take care of her in her old age. And my sisters, let me know all about them. I would write to them, and learn all I want to know of them, without disturbing you in any way, but that, through your unrighteous conduct, they have been entirely deprived of the power to read and write. You have kept them in utter ignorance, and have therefore robbed them of the sweet enjoyments of writing or receiving letters from absent friends and relatives. Your wickedness and cruelty committed in this respect on your fellow-creatures, are greater than all the stripes you have laid upon my back, or theirs. It is an outrage upon the soul—a war upon the immortal spirit, and one for which you must give account at the bar of our common Father and Creator.

*   *   *

I will now bring this letter to a close, you shall hear from me again unless you let me hear from you. I intend to make use of you as a weapon with which to assail the system of slavery—as a means of concentrating public attention on the system, and deepening their horror of trafficking in the souls and bodies of men. I shall make use of you as a means of exposing the character of the American church and clergy— and as a means of bringing this guilty nation with yourself to repentance. In doing this I entertain no malice towards you personally. There is no roof under which you would be more safe than mine, and there is nothing in my house which you might need for your comfort, which I would not readily grant. Indeed, I should esteem it a privilege, to set you an example as to how mankind ought to treat each other.

I am your fellow man, but not your slave,

Frederick Douglass.

—September 22, 1848

Ain't no way to keep us
down on no ground.
We just jump up, again
and again and again.

—**Ntozake Shange,** *poet*

Eternal vigilance is
the price of liberty . . .

—IDA B. WELLS, *writer*

You can't put liberty on the tip of the
lips and expect people not to drink it.

—**Josephine Baker**, *performer*

A person is a person because he recognizes others as persons.

—ARCHBISHOP DESMOND TUTU, *civil rights leader*

I never doubted my ability, but when you hear all your life you're inferior, it makes you wonder if the other guys have something you've never seen before. If they do, I'm still looking for it.

—**Hank Aaron**, *athlete*

"From Whence My Love of Freedom Sprung"

(EXCERPT FROM TO THE RIGHT HONOURABLE
WILLIAM, EARL OF DARTMOUTH, HIS MAJESTY'S
PRINCIPAL SECRETARY OF STATE FOR NORTH AMERICA)

PHILLIS WHEATLEY

A poetess who lived only thirty-one years, **Phillis Wheatley**
(c. 1753-1784) left a lasting mark on the people of her time.
The echo of her words is felt just as strongly today.

Hail, happy day, when, smiling like the morn,
Fair *Freedom* rose *New-England* to adorn:
The northern clime beneath her genial ray,
Dartmouth, congratulates thy blissful sway:
Elate with hope her race no longer mourns,

Each soul expands, each grateful bosom burns,
While in thine hand with pleasure we behold
The silken reins, and *Freedom*'s charms unfold.
Long lost to realms beneath the northern skies
She shines supreme, while hated *faction* dies:
Soon as appear'd the *Goddess* long desir'd,
Sick at the view, she languish'd and expir'd;
Thus from the splendors of the morning light
The owl in sadness seeks the caves of night.

No more *America*, in mournful strain
Of wrongs, and grievance unredress'd complain,
No longer shalt thou dread the iron chain,
Which wanton *Tyranny* with lawless hand
Had made, and with it meant t'enslave the land.

No more America,

Should you, my lord, while you peruse my song,
Wonder from whence my love of *Freedom* sprung,
Whence flow these wishes for the common good,
By feeling hearts alone best understood,
I, young in life, by seeming cruel fate
Was snatch'd from *Afric's* fancy'd happy seat:
What pangs excruciating must molest,
What sorrows labour in my parent's breast?
Steel'd was that soul and by no misery mov'd
That from a father seiz'd his babe belov'd:
Such, such my case. And can I then but pray
Others may never feel tyrannic sway?

✻　✻　✻

—1773

in mournful strain

I looked at my hands
to see if I was
the same person
now I was free.
There was such a glory
over everything,
the sun came like gold
through the trees,
and over the fields,
and I felt like
I was in heaven.

—**Harriet Tubman**, *former slave who led over 300*
others to freedom via the Underground Railroad

The struggle is my life.

—NELSON MANDELA, *South African patriot*

If something is yours by right,
then fight for it or shut up.
If you can't fight for it, then forget it.

—Malcolm X

People always say that I
didn't give up my seat
because I was tired, but that
isn't true. . . . No, the only
tired I was, was tired
of giving in.

—ROSA PARKS,

"The Mother of the Civil Rights Movement"

Ain't I a Woman?

(ADDRESS TO THE
WOMEN'S RIGHTS CONVENTION)

Sojourner Truth

When a minister declared in 1851 that only men should have
rights, as Jesus had been a man and not a woman, **Sojourner Truth**
(c. 1799-1883) responded with this speech at the Ohio Women's
Rights Convention. Although born a slave and given the name Isabella
Bomefree, she changed her name to Sojourner Truth in 1843, and
became an abolitionist and a leader in the women's rights movement.

Well, children, where there is so much racket
there must be somethin' out o'kilter. I think
that 'twixt the Negroes of the North and the
South and the women at the North, all talkin' 'bout rights,
the white men will be in a fix pretty soon. But what's all this
here talkin' 'bout?

That man over there say that women needs to be helped
into carriages, and lifted over ditches, and to have the best
place everywhere. Nobody ever helps me into carriages, or
over mud-puddles, or give me any best place! And ain't I a
woman? Look at me? Look at my arm! I have ploughed, and
planted, and gathered into barns, and no man could head
me! And ain't I a woman? I could work as much and eat as
much as a man—when I could get it—and bear the lash as

well! And ain't I a woman? I have borne thirteen children, and seen 'em mos' all sold off to slavery, and when I cried out with my mother's grief, none but Jesus heard me! And ain't I a woman?

Then they talk about this thing in the head; what's this they call it? ["Intellect," whispered someone near.] That's it honey. What's that got to do with women's rights or Negro's rights? If my cup won't hold but a pint and yours holds a quart, wouldn't you be mean not to let me have my little half measure full?

Then that little man in black there, he says women can't have as much rights as men, 'cause Christ wasn't a woman! Where did your Christ come from? Where did your Christ come from? From God and a woman! Man had nothin' to do with Him.

If the first woman God ever made was strong enough to turn the world upside down all alone, these women together ought to be able to turn it back, and get it right side up again? And now they is asking to do it, they better let 'em. 'Bliged to you for hearin' me, and now ole Sojourner hasn't got nothin' more to say.

—Akron, Ohio
May 29, 1851

"Am I a Man?"

(EXCERPT FROM SPEECH TO THE GEORGIA LEGISLATURE)

Henry M. Turner

The Bishop **Henry McNeal Turner** (1843-1915) was the chaplain of
the First United States Colored Troops during the Civil War. In 1868
he was elected a representative to the Georgia State Legislature. This
speech was written in response to his expulsion later that same year,
when the Legislature voted that African Americans were ineligible to
serve. He was reinstated in 1870.

☆   ☆   ☆

Whose Legislature is this? Is it a white man's
Legislature, or is it a black man's Legislature? Who
voted for a Constitutional Convention, in obedi-
ence to the mandate of the Congress of the United States? Who
first rallied around the standard of Reconstruction? Who set the
ball of loyalty rolling in the State of Georgia? And whose voice
was heard on the hills and in the valleys of this State? It was the

voice of the brawny-armed Negro, with the few humanitarian-hearted white men who came to our assistance. I claim the honor, sir, of having been the instrument of convincing hundreds—yea, thousands—of white men, that to reconstruct under the measures of the United States Congress was the safest and the best course for the interest of the State.

Let us look at some facts in connection with this matter. Did half the white men of Georgia vote for this Legislature? Did not the great bulk of them fight, with all their strength, the Constitution under which we are acting? And did they not fight against the organization of this Legislature? And further, sir, did they not *vote* against it? Yes, sir! And there are persons in this Legislature, to-day, who are ready to spit their poison in my face, while they themselves opposed, with all their power, the ratification of this Constitution. They question my right to a seat in this body, to represent the people whose legal votes elected me. This objection, sir, is an unheard of monopoly of power. No analogy can be found for it, except it be the case of a man who should go into my house, take possession of my wife and children, and then tell me to walk out. I stand very much in the position of a criminal before your bar, because I dare to be the exponent of the views of those who sent me here. Or, in other words, we are told that if black men want to speak, they must speak through white trumpets; if black men want their sentiments expressed, they must be adulterated and sent through white messengers, who will quibble, and equivocate, and evade, as rapidly as the pendulum of a clock. If this be not done, then the black men have committed an outrage, and their Representatives must be denied the right to represent their constituents.

The great question, sir, is this: Am I a man? If I am such, I claim the rights of a man. Am I not a man because I happen to be of a darker hue than honorable gentlemen around me?

* * *

But Mr. Speaker, I do not regard this movement as a thrust at me. It is a thrust at the Bible—a thrust at the God of the Universe, for making a man and not finishing him; it is simply calling the Great Jehovah a fool. Why, sir, though we are not white, we have accomplished much. We have pioneered civilization here; we have built up your country; we have worked in your fields, and garnered your harvests, for two hundred and fifty years! And what do we ask of you in return?

"The black man cannot protect a country, if the country doesn't protect him..."

43

Do we ask you for compensation for the sweat our fathers bore for you—for the tears you have caused, and the hearts you have broken, and the lives you have curtailed, and the blood you have spilled? Do we ask retaliation? We ask it not. We are willing to let the dead past bury its dead; but we ask you now for our RIGHTS. You have all the elements of superiority upon your side; you have our money and your own; you have our education and your own; and you have our land and your own, too. We, who number hundreds of thousands in Georgia, including our wives and families, with not a foot of land to call our own—strangers in the land of our birth; without money, without education, without aid, without a roof to cover us while we live, nor sufficient clay to cover us when we die! It is extraordinary that a race such as yours, professing gallantry, and chivalry, and education, and superiority, living in a land where ringing chimes call child and sire to the Church of God—a land where Bibles are read and Gospel truths are spoken, and where courts of justice are presumed to exist; it is extraordinary, I say, that, with all these advantages on your side, you can make war upon the poor defenseless black man.

✻   ✻   ✻

You may expel us, gentlemen, but I firmly believe that you will some day repent it. The black man cannot protect a country, if the country doesn't protect him. . . .

—September 3, 1868

Let
me
tell
you
something:
I
am
a
man.

—ALEX HALEY, *writer*
from *Roots*

So few of us can understand what it takes to make a man—the man who will never say die; the man who will never give up; the man who will never depend upon others to do for him what he ought to do for himself; the man who will not blame God, who will not blame Nature, who will not blame Fate for his condition; but the man who will go out and make conditions to suit himself.

—**Marcus Garvey,** *founder and leader of the*
UNIA (Universal Negro Improvement Association)

I am the kind of Negro that most white people don't know about. They either don't know, or maybe they don't *want* to know, . . . I mean just listen to that fella, David Duke, down in Louisiana—the fella that was with the Klan and then was going to run for president. . . . Well, I'm just as good an American as he is—better!

—**Bessie Delaney,** *teacher*
from ***Having Our Say***

I'm the man
you think
you are
. . . and if you
don't know
what I'll do,
figure out
what you'll do.
I'll do the same thing
—only more of it.

—MALCOLM X

On Being Black
W. E. B. Du Bois

One of the founders of the NAACP, **William Edward Burghardt Du Bois** (1868-1963) was an ardent advocate of education for African Americans. He believed the best-educated African Americans were duty-bound to lead the race forward. He also created the NAACP magazine *The Crisis*, which he edited for twenty-four years.

My friend, who is pale and positive, said to me yesterday, as the tired sun was nodding:

"You are too sensitive."

I admit, I am—sensitive. I am artificial. I cringe or am bumptious or immobile. I am intellectually dishonest, art-blind, and I lack humor.

"Why don't you stop all this?" she retorts triumphantly.

You will not let us.

"There you go again. You know that I—"

Wait! I answer. Wait!

I arise at seven. The milkman has neglected me. He pays little attention to colored districts. My white neighbor glares elaborately. I walk softly, lest I disturb him. The children jeer as I pass to work. The women in the street car withdraw their skirts or prefer to stand. The policeman is truculent. The elevator man hates to serve Negroes. My job is insecure because the white union wants it and does not want me. I try to lunch, but no place near will serve me. I go forty blocks to Marshall's, but the Committee of Fourteen closes Marshall's; they say that white women frequent it.

"Do all eating places discriminate?"

No, but how shall I know which do not—except—

I hurry home through crowds. They mutter or get angry. I go to a mass-meeting. They stare. I go to a church. "We don't admit niggers!"

Or perhaps I leave the beaten track. I seek new work. "Our employees would not work with you; our customers would object."

I ask to help in social uplift.

"Why—er—we will write you."

I enter the free field of science. Every laboratory door is closed and no endowments are available.

I seek the universal mistress, Art; the studio door is locked.

I write literature. "We cannot publish stories of colored folk of that type." It's the only type I know.

Pessimism is

This is my life. It makes me idiotic. It gives me artificial problems. I hesitate, I rush, I waver. In fine—I am sensitive!

My pale friend looks at me with disbelief and curling tongue.

"Do you mean to sit there and tell me that this is what happens to you each day?"

Certainly not, I answer low.

"Then you only fear it will happen?"

I fear!

"Well, haven't you the courage to rise above a—almost a craven fear?"

Quite—quite craven is my fear, I admit; but the terrible thing is—these things do happen!

"But you just said—"

They do happen. Not all each day—surely not. But now and then—now seldom; now, sudden; now after a week, now in a chain of awful minutes; not everywhere, but anywhere—in Boston, in Atlanta. That's the hell of it. Imagine spending your life looking for insults or for hiding places from them—shrinking (instinctively and despite desperate bolsterings of courage) from blows that are not always, but ever; not each day, but each week, each month, each year. Just, perhaps, as you have choked back the

cowardice.

craven fear and cried, "I am and will be the master of my—"

"No more tickets down stairs; here's one to the smoking gallery."

You hesitate. You beat back your suspicions. After all, a cigarette with Charlie Chaplin—then a white man pushes by—

"Three in the orchestra."

"Yes, sir." And in he goes.

Suddenly your heart chills. You turn yourself away toward the golden twinkle of the purple night and hesitate again. What's the use? Why not always yield—always take what's offered—always bow to force, whether of cannons or dislike? Then the great fear surges in your soul, the real fear—the fear beside which other fears are vain imaginings; the fear lest right there and then you are losing your own soul; that you are losing your own soul and the soul of a people; that millions of unborn children, black and gold and mauve, are being there and then despoiled by you because you are a coward and dare not fight!

Suddenly that silly orchestra seat and the cavorting of a comedian with funny feet become matters of life, death, and immortality; you grasp the pillars of the universe and strain as you sway back to that befrilled ticket girl. You grip your soul for riot and murder. You choke and sputter, and she, seeing that you are about to make a "fuss" obeys her orders and throws the tickets at you in contempt. Then you slink to your seat and crouch in the darkness before the film, with every tissue burning! The miserable wave of reaction engulfs you. To think of compelling puppies to take your hard-earned money; fattening hogs to hate you and yours; forcing your way among cheap and tawdry idiots—God! What a night of pleasure!

Why do not those who are scarred in the world's battle and hurt by its hardness travel to these places of beauty and drown themselves in the utter joy of life? I asked this once sitting in a Southern home. Outside, the spring of a Georgia February was luring gold to the bushes and languor to the soft air. Around me sat color in human flesh—brown that crimsoned readily; dim soft-yellow that escaped description; cream-like duskiness that shadowed to rich tints of autumn leaves. And yet a suggested journey in the world brought no response.

"I should think you would like to travel," said the white one.

But no, the thought of a journey seemed to depress them.

Did you ever see a "Jim-Crow" waiting-room? There are always exceptions, as at Greensboro—but usually there is no heat in winter and no air in summer; with undisturbed loafers and train hands and broken, disreputable settees; to buy a ticket is torture;

you stand and stand and wait and wait until every white person at the "other window" is waited on. Then the tired agent yells across, because all the tickets and money are over there—

"What d' y'e want? What? Where?"

The agent browbeats and contradicts you, hurries and confuses the ignorant, gives many persons the wrong change, compels some to purchase their tickets on the train at a higher price, and sends you and me out on the platform burning with indignation and hatred!

The "Jim-Crow" car is up next the baggage car and engine. It stops out beyond the covering in the rain or sun or dust. Usually there is no step to help you climb on, and often the car is a smoker cut in two, and you must pass through the white smokers or else they pass through your part, with swagger and noise and stares. Your compartment is a half or a quarter or an eighth of the oldest car in service on the road. Unless it happens to be a through express, the plush is caked with dirt, the floor is grimy, and the windows dirty. An impertinent white newsboy occupies two seats at the end of the car and importunes you to the point of rage to buy cheap candy, Coca-Cola, and worthless, if not vulgar, books. He yells and swaggers, while a continued stream of white men saunters back and forth from the smoker, to buy and hear. The white train crew from the baggage car uses the "Jim-Crow" to lounge in and perform their toilet. The conductor appropriates two seats for himself and his papers and yells gruffly for your tickets almost before the train has started. It is best not to ask him for information even in the gentlest tones. His information is for white persons chiefly. It is difficult to get lunch or clean water. Lunch rooms either don't serve niggers or serve them at some dirty and ill-attended hole in the wall. As for toilet rooms—don't! If you have to change cars, be wary of junctions which are usually without accommodation and filled with quarrelsome white persons who hate a "darky dressed up." You are apt to have the company of a sheriff and a couple of meek or sullen black prisoners on part of your way and dirty colored section hands will pour in toward night and drive you to the smallest corner.

"No," said the little lady in the corner (she looked like an ivory cameo and her dress flowed on her like a caress), "we don't travel much."

Pessimism is cowardice. The man who cannot frankly acknowledge "Jim-Crow" car as a fact and yet live and hope is simply afraid either of himself or of the world. There is not in the world a more disgraceful denial of human brotherhood than the "Jim-Crow" car of the southern United States; but, too, just as true, there is nothing more beautiful in the universe than sunset and moonlight on Montego Bay in far Jamaica. And both things are true and both belong to this, our world, and neither can be denied.... — February 18, 1920

Last time I was down South
I walked into this restaurant,
and this white waitress came
up to me and said:

"We don't serve colored
people here."

I said:

"That's all right,
I don't eat colored people.
Bring me a whole fried
chicken."

—DICK GREGORY, *comedian and political activist*
from *Nigger: An Autobiography*

"What color is God's spirit?"
"It doesn't have a color," she said.
"God is the color of water.
Water doesn't have a color."

—James McBride, *writer*
from *The Color of Water*

I want to be black, to know black, to luxuriate
in whatever I might be calling blackness at any
particular time—but to do so in order to come
out the other side, to experience a humanity that
is neither colorless nor reducible to color.

—HENRY LOUIS GATES JR., *writer and scholar*

one love

—Bob Marley, *musician*

It doesn't matter who you are,
where you come from.
The ability to triumph begins
with you. Always.

—OPRAH WINFREY,
The Queen of All Media

I wanna let young people know that it is NOT A BURDEN to love [God] and to represent Him, and to be who you are, as fly and as hot and as whatever and to still love God and to serve Him. It is not a contradiction.
IT IS NOT A CONTRADICTION.

—**Lauryn Hill,** *musician*

What makes you really happy is when you love and give and understand, when you look at beauty and really see it. We are so busy watching the road under our feet we forget to look up at the beauty all around us. —**Dorothy Dandridge**, *actress*

There is always some beauty in life. Look up . . . and get on with it. Build you a rainbow. Do it yourself! If you can't do that, build your mind near one. Learn how to fly. Then . . . soar a little.

—J. CALIFORNIA COOPER, *writer*
from "**Do-It-Yourself Rainbow**"

Learning to Read
Frances E. W. Harper

Very soon the Yankee teachers
    Came down and set up school;
But, oh! how the Rebs did hate it,—
    It was agin' their rule.

Our masters always tried to hide
    Book learning from our eyes;
Knowledge didn't agree with slavery—
    'Twould make us all too wise.

But some of us would try to steal
    A little from the book,
And put the words together,
    And learn by hook or crook.

I remember Uncle Caldwell,
    Who took pot liquor fat
And greased the pages of his book,
    And hid it in his hat.

And had his master ever seen
　　　　The leaves upon his head,
He'd have thought them greasy papers,
　　　　But nothing to be read.

And there was Mr. Turner's Ben,
　　　　Who heard the children spell,
And picked the words right up by heart,
　　　　And learned to read 'em well.

Well, the Northern folks kept sending
　　　　The Yankee teachers down;
And they stood right up and helped us,
　　　　Though Rebs did sneer and frown.

And, I longed to read my Bible,
　　　　For precious words it said;
But when I begun to learn it,
　　　　Folks just shook their heads,

And said there is no use trying,
　　　　Oh! Chloe, you're too late;

But as I was rising sixty,
        I had no time to wait.

So I got a pair of glasses,
        And straight to work I went,
And never stopped till I could read
        The hymns and Testament.

Then I got a little cabin—
        A place to call my own—
And I felt as independent
        As the queen upon her throne.

Frances Ellen Watkins Harper (1825-1911) was the first female instructor at the Ohio Union Seminary, which later became Wilberforce University. She was an active member of the Underground Railroad, a suffragette, and the founder of the National Association of Colored Women.

And had his master
　　ever seen
The leaves upon
　　his head,
He'd have thought
　　them greasy papers,
But nothing to be read.

Education is the key to unlock the golden door of freedom.

—GEORGE WASHINGTON CARVER,
scientist

Getting the degree meant more to me than an NCAA title, being named All-American, or winning an Olympic Gold Medal.

—**Patrick Ewing**, *athlete*

Do not call for Black power or green power. Call for brainpower.

—BARBARA JORDAN, CONGRESSWOMAN

If you're the smartest person you know, you have a problem.

—Nikki Giovanni, *poet*

I listened, I was aware of my success, but I never stopped trying to get better.

—Michael Jordan, athlete

Find the power. Find the Queen who lives inside of you, embrace her, nourish her, praise her, hold her accountable, and love her. Become her.

— **Queen Latifah,** *musician and actress*

from *Ladies First*

Nothing is going to be handed to you. You have to make things happen.

—**Florence Griffith Joyner**, *athlete*

"What Are We Worth?"

(EXCERPT FROM A VOICE FROM THE SOUTH)

Anna Julia Cooper

Ostracized by African American leaders because of her gender and by
suffragettes because of her race, Dr. **Anna Julia Cooper** (1856-1961)
nonetheless continued to speak in the only voice she could: that of the
African American female. At a time when women did not have the vote
and black women were not accorded respect, Dr. Cooper was ahead of
her time and clear as a bell.

*　　*　　*

In the heart of what is known as the "Black Belt"
of Alabama and within easy reach of the great cotton
plantations of Georgia, Mississippi, and Florida, a
devoted young colored man ten years ago started a school

"A sound manhood, a true womanhood is a fruit which the lowliest can grow."

with about thirty Negro children assembled in a comical looking shanty at Tuskegee. His devotion was contagious and his work grew; an abandoned farm of 100 acres was secured and that gradually grew to 640 acres, largely wood-land, on which a busy and prosperous school is located; and besides a supply farm was added, of heavy rich land, 800 acres, from which grain and sugar cane are main products. Since 1881, 2,947 students have been taught here, of whom 102 have graduated, while 200 more have received enough training to fit them to do good work as teachers, intelligent farmers, and mechanics. The latest enrollment shows girls, 247; boys, 264. Of the 102 graduates, 70 percent are teachers, ministers, and farmers. They usually combine teaching and farming. Three are printers (learned the trades at school), one is a tinner, one a blacksmith, one a wheel-wright, three are merchants, three are carpenters, others in the professions, or filling miscellaneous positions.

That man is paying his debt by giving to this country *living, working, consecrated men and women!*

Now each can give something. It may not be a poem, or marble bust, or fragrant flower even; it may not be ours to place our lives on the altar of country as a loving sacrifice, or even to devote our living activities so extensively as B. T. Washington to supplying the world's need for strong and willing helpers. But we can at least *give ourselves.* Each can be *one* of those strong willing helpers—even though nature has denied him the talent of endlessly multiplying his force. And nothing less can honorably cancel our debt. Each is under a most sacred obligation not to squander the material committed to him, not to sap its strength in folly and vice, and to see at the least that he delivers a product worthy the labor and cost which have been expended on him. A sound manhood, a true womanhood is a fruit which the lowliest can grow. And it is a com-modity of which the supply never exceeds the demand.

There is no danger of the market being glutted. The world will always want *men*. The worth of one is infinite. To this value all other values are merely relative. Our money, our schools, our governments, our free institutions, our systems of religion and forms of creeds are all first and last to be judged by this standard: what sort of men and women do they grow? How are men and women being shaped and molded by this system of training, under this or that form of government, by this or that standard of moral action? You propose a new theory of education; *what sort of men does it turn out?* Does your system make boys and girls superficial and mechanical? Is it a producing of average percentages or a rounding out of manhood—a sound, thorough, and practical development—or a scramble for standing and marks?

We have a notion here in America that our political institutions—the possibilities of a liberal and progressive democracy, founded on universal suffrage and in some hoped-for, providential way *compelling* universal education and devotion—our peculiar American attainments are richly worth all they have cost in blood and anguish. But our form of government, divinely ordered as we dream it to be, must be brought to the bar to be tested by this standard. It is nothing worth of itself—independently of whether it furnishes a good atmosphere in which to cultivate men. Is it developing a self respecting freedom, a sound manliness on the part of *the individual*—or does it put into the power of the wealthy few the opportunity and the temptation to corrupt the many? If our vaunted *"rule of the people"* does not breed nobler men and women than monarchies have done—it must and will inevitably give place to something better.

I care not for the theoretical symmetry and impregnable logic of your moral code, I care not for the hoary respectability and traditional mysticisms of your theological institutions, I care not for the beauty and solemnity of your rituals and religious ceremonies, I care not even for the reasonableness and unimpeachable fairness of your social ethics—if it does not turn out better, nobler, truer men and women—if it does not add to the world's stock of valuable souls—if it does not give us a sounder, healthier, more reliable product from this great factory of *men*—I will have none of it. I shall not try to test your logic, but weigh your results—and that test is the *measure of the stature of the fullness*

"And the world—our world, will surely and unerringly see us as we are."

of a man. You need not formulate and establish the credibility and authenticity of Christian Evidences, when you can demonstrate and prove the present value of CHRISTIAN MEN. And this test for systems of belief, for schools of thought, and for theories of conduct, is also the ultimate and inevitable test of nations, of races, and of individuals. What sort of men do you turn out? *How* are you supplying the great demands of the world's market? What is your true value?

This, we may be sure, will be the final test by which the colored man in America will one day be judged in the cool, calm, unimpassioned, unprejudiced second thought of the American people.

Let us then quietly commend ourselves to this higher court—this final tribunal. Short sighted idiosyncrasies are but transient phenomena. It is futile to combat them, and unphilosophical to be depressed by them. To allow such things to overwhelm us, or even to absorb undue thought, is an admission of weakness. As sure as time is—*these mists will clear away*. And the world—our world, will surely and unerringly see us as we are. Our only care need be the intrinsic worth of our contributions. If we represent the ignorance and poverty, the vice and destructiveness, the vagabondism and parasitism in the world's economy, no amount of philanthropy and benevolent sentiment can win for us esteem: and if we contribute a positive value in those things the world prizes, no amount of negrophobia can ultimately prevent its recognition. And our great "problem" after all is to be solved not by brooding over it, and orating about it, but by *living into it*.

—1892

Mama may have
Papa may have
But God bless the child
that's got his own.

—**Billie Holiday**, *singer*

It is easy to be independent when you've got money. But to be independent when you haven't got a thing—that's the Lord's test.

—**Mahalia Jackson**, *gospel singer*

The tired among us must recharge their batteries. The uninitiated must learn and gird their loins. We have not finished the job of making our country whole.

—**James Farmer**, *civil rights leader and a founder of CORE (Congress of Racial Equality)*

I
am sail-
ing into the
wind and the dark.
But I am doing my
best to keep my boat steady
and my sails full.

—ARTHUR ASHE, *athlete*

"... just tell the tale,
you little honeys."

—Toni Cade Bambara, *writer*
from *Deep Sightings and Rescue Missions*

From a Black Woman to a Black Man

Maya Angelou

Maya Angelou (1928 -   ), Pulitzer Prize–winner and first African
American streetcar conductor in San Francisco, wrote this balm of
healing especially for the Million Man March. It is a poem of forgive-
ness for an accusation never made, a renewal of a vow of mutual
respect between African American men and women.

The night has been long
The wounds have been deep
The pit has been dark
The walls have been steep

Beneath a blue sky
On a golden beach
I was dragged by braids
Beyond your reach

Your hands were tied
Your feet were bound
You couldn't save me
From the selling ground

We lay in the slave hold
Air thickened with cries
You lowered your head
Evading my eyes

The night has been long
The wounds have been deep
The pit has been dark
The walls have been steep

We stood on the block
Clothed only in shame
Then someone whispered
That we were to blame

If our skin had been pale
And our hair had been straight
We would have escaped
Our devilish fate

Our lives have been shaped
By that crippling lie
Yet, you were not guilty
And neither was I

The night has been long
The wounds have been deep
The pit has been dark
The walls have been steep

Today we declare
This a guilt free season
Greed was the culprit
Greed was the reason.

Voices of old, spirit sound
Speak to us in words profound
Across the years and centuries
Across the oceans and rolling seas

"Draw near to each other
Value your race
You were paid for dearly
In another place.

The hell you have lived through
And live through still
Has sharpened your senses
And toughened your will."

The night has been long
The wounds have been deep
The pit has been dark
The walls have been steep

I look through your anguish
Down into your soul
And know that together
We can be made whole.

I look through the posture
And past your disguise
And see pride of race
In your big brown eyes.

Clap hands
Together at this meeting ground

Clap hands
We have dallied over long
On the low road of indifference

Clap hands
Let us come together
And reveal our hearts

Clap hands
Let us revive our spirits

Clap hands
Let us cleanse our souls
Let us leave the preening as
Impostors in our history

Clap hands
And call our spirits back from the ledge

Clap hands
Call joy back into our conversation

Clap hands
Call laughter back into our dialogue

Clap hands
Call nurturing back into our nurseries
And romance back into our bedrooms

The ancestors tell us
Through a history of pain
We're a going on people
On the rise again

Make a vow of friendship
Let us take each other's hand
Shout Hurray for the Black Woman
Shout Hurray for the Black Man

Poem penned and read at Million Man March,
October 16, 1995.

They held each other up.
They patted each other's
back as if each had
fallen and scraped a knee
and had no one else
to turn to for comfort.
It seemed as if they
hugged each other
for the past and
for the future.

—**Terry McMillan,** *writer*
from ***Mama***

I don't allow anyone to put a limit on my dreaming, and I dream big. Always.

—GORDON PARKS, *photographer*

Today, let us become aware of the healing power within and dedicate ourselves to uplifting those we touch.

—Iyanla Vanzant, *motivational writer*

We must always attempt to lift as we climb.

—**Angela Y. Davis**,
civil rights activist

The Pledge
The Million Man March Oath

I (*say your name*) pledge that from this day forward I will strive to love my brother, as I love myself.

I (*say your name*) pledge that from this day forward I will strive to improve myself spiritually, morally, mentally, socially, politically, and economically for the benefit of myself, my family, and my people.

I (*say your name*) pledge that I will strive to build businesses, build houses, build hospitals, build factories, and enter into international trade for the good of myself, my family, and my people.

I (*say your name*) pledge that from this day forward I will never raise my hand with a knife or a gun to beat, cut, or shoot any member of my family, or any human being except in self-defense.

I (*say your name*) pledge that from this day forward I will never abuse my wife by striking her, or disrespecting her, for she is the mother of my children, and the producer of my future.

I (*say your name*) pledge that from this day forward I will never engage in the abuse of children, little boys, or little girls for sexual gratification, but I will let them grow in peace to be strong men and women for the future of our people.

I (*say your name*) will never again use the "B" word to describe any female but particularly my own black sister.

I (*say your name*) pledge that from this day forward I will not poison my body with drugs or that which is destructive to my health or to my well-being.

I (*say your name*) pledge that from this day forward I will support black newspapers, black radio, and black television. I will support black artists who clean up their act, show respect for themselves, respect for their people, and respect for the heirs of the human family.

I (*say your name*) will do all of this, so help me God.

The Million Man March, organized by Nation of Islam leader Louis Farrakhan, took place on October 16, 1995, in Washington, D.C. Also known as a Day of Atonement, it was attended by 870,000 strong, while several times that many African American men made this pledge from wherever they were that day.

I thought "Should should I yell, or should I cry?"

And I guess ended up doing them all.

—**Serena Williams,** *on winning U.S. Open*

You are a reflection
of your people—regardless
of what anybody says.

—**Haki Madhubuti**, *poet and writer*

It made me wann

—**Nathan McCall,** *writer and journalist*
from ***Makes Me Wanna Holler: A Young Black Man in America***

SCREAM,

We are the African and the trader.
We are the Indian and the settler.
We are the slaver and the enslaved.
We are oppressor and oppressed.
We are the women and we are the men.
We are the children.

—**Alice Walker**, *writer*

There are rebels and there are innovators. I'm an innovator.

—LL COOL J, *rap artist and actor*

holler . . .

Role models can be black. Role models can be white. Role models can be generals. Role models can be principals, teachers, doctors, or just your parent who brought you into this world and who is trying to give you the best of everything.

—COLIN POWELL, *four-star general*
AND FORMER HEAD OF THE JOINT CHIEFS OF STAFF
OF THE U.S. ARMED FORCES

There's different ways that you can measure people's greatness. And the way I like to measure greatness is: How many people do you affect? In your time on this earth, how many people can you affect? How many people can you make want to be better? Or how many people can you inspire to do what you do?

—**Will Smith**, *actor and singer*

"Our Time Has Come"

(Excerpt from the July 19, 1984,
Address Before the
Democratic National Convention)

Jesse Jackson

The Reverend **Jesse Louis Jackson** (1941-   ), founder of Operation
PUSH and the Rainbow Coalition, brought the house down and
Americans to their feet with this address in 1984. He was to perform
a similar feat later at the 1988 Democratic National Convention. But
in 1984 his call was to young America.

I have a message for our youth. I challenge them to put
hope in their brains and not dope in their veins. I told
them that like Jesus, I, too, was born in the slum, and
just because you're born in a slum does not mean the slum is
born in you and you can rise above it if your mind is made
up. I told them in every slum there are two sides. When I see
a broken window that's the slummy side. Train some youth
to become a glazier; that is the sunny side. When I see a
missing brick, that is the slummy side. Let that child in a
union and become a brick mason and build; that is the sunny
side. When I see a missing door, that is the slummy side.
Train some youth to become a carpenter, that is the sunny

"We come from disgrace to amazing grace."

side. When I see the vulgar words and hieroglyphics of destitution on the walls, that is the slummy side. Train some youth to be a painter and artist, that is the sunny side.

We leave this place looking for the sunny side because there's a brighter side somewhere. I am more convinced than ever that we can win. We will vault up the rough side of the mountain. We can win. I just want young America to do me one favor, just one favor.

Exercise the right to dream. You must face reality, that which is. But then dream of a reality that ought to be, that must be. Live beyond the pain of reality with the dream of a bright tomorrow. Use hope and imagination as weapons of survival and progress. Use love to motivate you and obligate you to serve the human family.

Young America, dream. Choose the human race over the nuclear race. Bury the weapons and don't bury the people. Dream—dream of a new value system. Teachers who teach for life and not just for a living; teach because they can't help it. Dream of lawyers more concerned about justice than a judgeship. Dream of doctors more concerned about public health than personal wealth. Dream of preachers and priests who will prophesy and not just profiteer. Preach and dream! Our time has come. Our time has come.

Suffering breeds character. Character breeds faith, and in the end faith will not disappoint. Our time has come. Our faith, hope, and dreams have prevailed. Our time has come. Weeping has endured for nights but that joy cometh in the morning.

Our time has come. No grave can hold our body down. Our time has come. No lie can live forever. Our time has come. We must leave the racial battle ground and come to the economic common ground and moral higher ground. America, our time has come.

We come from disgrace to amazing grace. Our time has come. Give me your tired, give me your poor, your huddled masses who yearn to breathe free and come November, there will be a change because our time has come.

Practice without thought is blind;
thought without practice is empty.

—**Kwame Nkrumah,** *first president*
of the Republic of Ghana

If a man is not faithful to his own individuality, he cannot be loyal to anybody.

—**Claude McKay**, *writer*

The past is a ghost,
the future a dream,
and all we ever have is now.

—**Bill Cosby**, *actor and comedian*

I Have a Dream
Martin Luther King Jr.

Winner of the 1964 Nobel Peace Prize for his steadfast policy of
nonviolent protest and the most prominent leader of the Civil Rights
movement in the twentieth century, Dr. **Martin Luther King Jr.**
(1929-1968) delivered this speech on August 28, 1963, as the keynote
speaker at the March in Washington, D.C. His birthday, January 15,
became a national holiday in 1986.

Five score years ago, a great American, in whose symbolic shadow we stand, signed the Emancipation Proclamation. This momentous decree came as a great beacon light of hope to millions of Negro slaves who had been seared in the flames of withering injustice. It came as a joyous daybreak to end the long night of captivity.

But one hundred years later, we must face the tragic fate that the Negro is still not free. One hundred years later, the life of the Negro is still sadly crippled by the manacles of segregation and the chains of discrimination. One hundred years later, the Negro lives on a lonely island of poverty in the midst of a vast ocean of material prosperity. One hundred years later the Negro is still languishing in the corners of American society and finds himself an exile in his own land. So we have come here today to dramatize an appalling condition.

> **"Now is the time to open the doors of opportunity to all of God's children."**

In a sense we have come to our nation's Capitol to cash a check. When the architects of our republic wrote the magnificent words of the Constitution and the Declaration of Independence, they were signing a promissory note to which every American was to fall heir. This note was a promise that all men would be guaranteed the inalienable rights of life, liberty, and the pursuit of happiness.

It is obvious today that America has defaulted on this promissory note insofar as her citizens of color are concerned. Instead of honoring this sacred obligation, America has given the Negro people a bad check; a check which has come back marked "insufficient funds." But we refuse to believe that the bank of justice is bankrupt. We refuse to believe that there are insufficient funds in the great vaults of opportunity of this nation. So we have come to cash this check—a check that will give us upon demand the riches of freedom and the security of justice.

We have also come to this hallowed spot to remind America of the fierce urgency of now. This is no time to engage in the luxury of cooling off or to take the tranquilizing drug of gradualism. Now is the time to make real the promises of Democracy. Now is the time to rise from the dark and desolate valley of segregation to the sunlit path of racial justice. Now is the time to open the doors of opportunity to all of God's children. Now is the time to lift our nation from the quicksands of racial injustice to the solid rock of brotherhood.

It would be fatal for the nation to overlook the urgency of the moment and to underestimate the determination of the Negro. This sweltering summer of the Negro's legitimate discontent will not pass until there is an invigorating autumn of freedom and equality. Nineteen sixty-three is not an end, but a beginning. Those who hope that the Negro needed to blow off steam and will now be content will have a rude awakening if the Nation returns to business as usual. There will be neither rest nor tranquility in America until the Negro is granted his citizenship rights. The whirlwinds of revolt will continue to shake the foundations of our Nation until the bright day of justice emerges.

But there is something that I must say to people who stand on the warm threshold which leads into the palace of justice.

"I have a dream that one day this nation will rise up and live out the true meaning of its creed"

In the process of gaining our rightful place we must not be guilty of wrongful deeds. Let us not seek to satisfy our thirst for freedom by drinking from the cup of bitterness and hatred. We must forever conduct our struggle on the high plane of dignity and discipline. We must not allow our creative protest to degenerate into physical violence. Again and again we must rise to the majestic heights of meeting physical force with soul force.

The marvelous new militancy which has engulfed the Negro community must not lead us to a distrust of all white people, for many of our white brothers, as evidenced by their presence here today, have come to realize that their destiny is tied up with our destiny and their freedom is inextricably bound to our freedom. We cannot walk alone.

And as walk, we must make the pledge that we shall march ahead. We cannot turn back. There are those who are asking the devotees of civil rights, "When will you be satisfied?"

We can never be satisfied as long as the Negro is the victim of the unspeakable horrors of police brutality. We can never be satisfied as long as our bodies, heavy with the fatigue of travel, cannot gain lodging in the motels of the highways and the hotels of the cities.

We cannot be satisfied as long as the Negro's basic mobility is from a smaller ghetto to a larger one. We can never be satisfied as long as a Negro in Mississippi cannot vote and a Negro in New York believes he has nothing for which to vote. No, no we are not satisfied, and we will not be satisfied until justice rolls down like waters and righteousness like a mighty stream.

I am not unmindful that some of you have come here out of great trials and tribulations. Some of you have come fresh from narrow jail cells. Some of you have come from areas where your quest for freedom left you battered by the storm of persecution and staggered by the winds of police brutality. Continue to work with the faith that unearned suffering is redemptive.

Go back to Mississippi, go back to Alabama, go back to South Carolina, go back to Georgia, go back to Louisiana, go back to the slums and ghettos of the Northern cities, knowing that somehow this situation can and will be changed. Let us not wallow in the valley of despair.

I say to you today, my friends, that in spite of the difficulties and frustrations of the moment I still have a dream. It is a dream deeply rooted in the American dream.

I have a dream that one day this nation will rise up and live out the true meaning of its creed: "We hold these truths to be self-evident; that all men are created equal."

I have a dream that one day on the red hills of Georgia the sons of former slaves and the sons of former slaveowners will be able to sit down together at the table of brotherhood.

I have a dream that one day even the state of Mississippi, a desert state sweltering with the heat of injustice and oppression, will be transformed into an oasis of freedom and justice.

I have a dream that my four children will one day live in a nation where they will not be judged by the color of their skin but by the content of their character.

I have a dream today.

I have a dream that one day the state of Alabama, whose governor's lips are presently dripping with the words of interposition and nullification, will be transformed into a situation where little black boys and black girls will be able to join hands with little white boys and white girls and walk together as sisters and brothers.

I have a dream today.

I have a dream that one day every valley shall be exalted, every hill and mountain shall be made low, the rough places will be made plains, and the crooked places will be made straight, and the glory of the Lord shall be revealed, and all flesh shall see it together.

"Free at last! free at last! thank God almighty, we are free at last!"

This is our hope. This is the faith with which I return to the South. With this faith we will be able to hew out of the mountain of despair a stone of hope. With this faith we will be able to transform the jangling discords of our nation into a beautiful symphony of brotherhood.

With this faith we will be able to work together, to pray together, to struggle together, to go to jail together, to stand up for freedom together, knowing that we will be free one day.

This will be the day when all of God's children will be able to sing with new meaning, "My country 'tis of thee, sweet land of liberty of thee I sing. Land where my fathers died, land of the pilgrim's pride, from every mountainside, let freedom ring."

And if America is to be a great nation this must become true. So let freedom ring from the prodigious hilltops of New Hampshire. Let freedom ring from the mighty mountains of New York. Let freedom ring from the heightening Alleghenies of Pennsylvania!

Let freedom ring from the snowcapped Rockies of Colorado!

Let freedom ring from the curvaceous peaks of California!

But not only that; let freedom ring from Stone Mountain of Georgia!

Let freedom ring from Lookout Mountain of Tennessee!

Let freedom ring from every hill and molehill of Mississippi. From every mountainside, let freedom ring.

When we let freedom ring, when we let it ring from every village and every hamlet, from every state and every city, we will be able to speed up that day when all of God's children, black men and white men, Jews and Gentiles, Protestants and Catholics, will be able to join hands and sing in the words of the old Negro spiritual, "Free at last! free at last! thank God almighty, we are free at last!"

—August 28, 1963

Know whence
you came.
If you know
whence you came,
there is really
no limit to
where you
can go.

—James Baldwin, *writer*
from *The Fire Next Time*

SELECT BIBLIOGRAPHY &
SUGGESTED READINGS

Altman, Susan. *Encyclopedia of African-American Heritage.* New York: Facts on File, 1997.

Ashe, Arthur, and Arnold Rampersad. *Days of Grace: A Memoir.* New York: Ballantine Books, 1993.

Baker, Jean-Claude, and Chris Chase. *Josephine: The Hungry Heart.* New York: Random House, 1993.

Bogle, Donald. *Dorothy Dandridge: A Biography.* New York: St. Martin's Press, 1997.

Boyd, Herb, and Robert L. Allen (eds.). *Brotherman: The Odyssey of Black Men in America.* New York: Ballantine Books, 1995.

Busby, Margaret (ed.). *Daughters of Africa: An International Anthology of Words and Writings by Women of African Descent.* New York: Random House, 1992.

Copage, Eric V. *Black Pearls: Daily Meditations, Affirmations, and Inspirations for African-Americans.* New York: Quill, 1993.

Dinwiddie-Boyd, Elza. *In Our Own Words: A Treasury of Quotations from the African-American Community.* New York: Avon Books, 1996.

Farmer, James. *Lay Bare the Heart: An Autobiography of the Civil Rights Movement.* New York: Arbor House, 1985.

Gates, Henry Louis. *Colored People: A Memoir.* New York: Knopf, 1994.

Hurston, Zora Neale. *I Love Myself: When I Am Laughing... and Then Again When I Am Looking Mean and Impressive,* ed. by Alice Walker. New York: The Feminist Press, 1979.

Jacques-Garvey, Amy (ed.). *Philosophy and Opinions of Marcus Garvey.* New York: Atheneum, 1992.

Killens, John Oliver, and Jerry W. Ward Jr. (eds.). *Black Southern Voices: An Anthology of Fiction, Poetry, Drama, Nonfiction, and Critical Essays.* New York: Penguin, 1992.

Mullane, Deirdre (ed.). *Words to Make My Dream Children Live: A Book of African American Quotations.* New York: Anchor Books, 1995.

Patterson, Katheryn. *No Time for Tears.* Chicago: Johnson, 1965.

Riley, D. Winbush (ed.). *My Soul Looks Back, 'Less I Forget: A Collection of Quotations by People of Color.* New York: HarperCollins, 1991.

Vanzant, Iyanla. *Acts of Faith: Daily Meditations for People of Color.* New York: Fireside, 1993.

About the Editors

Stephen Patterson is a playwright and book critic. His plays include *What Do White People Be Thinking?*, *Boo! Seven Characters, No Guarantees*, and *All About Steve: Musings of an Ebony Queer.* He is currently completing a book of short stories, *The Watermelon Don't Roll Far from the Vine.*

S. M. Wu is an acquisitions editor and project editor. She has edited such titles as *African Folktales*, Kate Chopin's *The Awakening*, *Irish Lore and Legends*, *Legends and Lore of the American Indians*, and *The Wit and Wisdom of Benjamin Franklin.* She is currently working on several short story anthologies.